Oceans Apart

A Guide to Maintaining Family Ties at a Distance

Oceans Apart

A Guide to Maintaining Family Ties at a Distance

Rochel U. Berman

Ktav Publishing House, Inc.
Jersey City, New Jersey

Library of Congress Cataloging-in-Publication Data

Berman, Rochel U.
 Oceans apart : a guide to maintaining family ties at a distance / Rochel U. Berman.
    p. cm.
 ISBN 978-1-60280-158-5
 1. Families. 2. Interpersonal communication. 3. Interpersonal relations. 4. Technological innovations--Social aspects. I. Title.
 HQ519.B47 2010
 306.87--dc22
                          2010020754

                       Published by
               KTAV Publishing House, Inc.
                   930 Newark Avenue
                  Jersey City, NJ 07306
                    bernie@ktav.com
                     www.ktav.com
                    (201) 963-9524
                  Fax (201) 963-0102

            Cover: GreenHouse Design Inc.

The ocean evokes longing,
while the bridge suggests connection.
I hope that readers will find a bridge
that keeps them connected to distant family members

R.B.

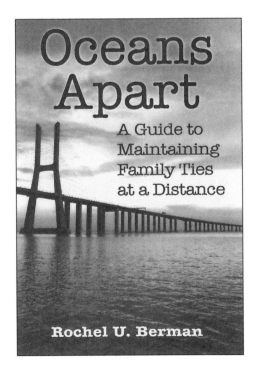

To

Amichai, Binyamin, Yakir and Ayelet

Oceans apart
Always in my heart

Contents

Contents

Contents

Acknowledgments

I first discussed the idea of this book with my longtime friend and colleague, Dr. Mary Noberini, associate professor of psychology at Manhattan College. Her immediate enthusiasm validated my interest and propelled me to move forward. Mary's global view of family issues informed my thinking and ultimately the way in which I framed the topic. She has been a guiding light throughout the process—carefully reviewing the manuscript and offering thoughtful suggestions. I am deeply indebted to her for her vision and for giving unstintingly of her time, guidance, and wisdom.

All those who agreed to be interviewed provided the material and substance from which I was able to mold this work. I am genuinely grateful to them for entrusting me with their moving and often heroic stories. Their experiences— most of which they articulated for the first time—were indispensable to the development of the subject matter. To ensure their anonymity, I have withheld their complete names and other minor biographical information.

There are a number of people and institutions whose advice I sought on a variety of matters. Many thanks to Penny Pearlman, an early-childhood specialist who provided tips on how to interview young children; to Rhonda Miller, a journalist who made valuable comments on the tone and style of the book; and to Carol Kahn, Hensha Gansbourg, Faye Kranz Greene, Rabbi Ovi Jacobs, and Professor Froma Zeitlin, who recommended people from the far corners of the world for me to interview. I also acknowledge the assistance of Chana Piekarski of the Chabad Shluchim office in New York, as well as Yael Katsman of Nefesh B'Nefesh in Israel and the St. Andrew's Episcopal Church in Boca Raton, Florida for introducing me to the Cox/Wenzel/ McGregor families, whose lives are committed to Christian missionary service in Madagascar. I am profoundly grateful to Joy Epstein, clinical supervisor, Department of Guidance and Community Resources at Nefesh B'Nefesh, for her insightful Foreword.

My close circle of friends, all of whom are oceans apart, long-distance grandmothers, were supportive and helpful throughout. I appreciate the sage counsel of Dina Drazin, Naomi Cohen, Debbie Petrover, Hassia Yehuda, and Judy Zemel.

My family was a vital part of the development of this book. My husband, George, who enhances and strengthens all that I do, kindly agreed to author Chapter 7, "Creative Uses of Technology." Readers will surely find his knowledge, expertise, and ideas helpful in maintaining family ties at a distance.

It is the challenges we have faced since our son, Josh, decided to move to Israel twenty years ago that motivated me to explore this topic. Through a series of heartwarming e-mails, his wife, Michal, has shared a wealth of information on how she has kept us alive in the minds and hearts of our grandchildren, even though we are not a physical presence in their lives. This interchange of thoughts and memories has served to strengthen the ongoing bond between us. Thanks, Michal.

When I first undertook this project, I had not thought to include sibling relationships at a distance as a topic. I am grateful to our son, Jonathan, for having pointed out the importance of this family tie and for sharing with me his thoughts and insights. I also express my appreciation to his wife, Monica, who carefully read several key chapters and offered incisive and provocative comments that helped clarify my thinking on key issues. Finally, I acknowledge with thanks the support and interest of my brother, Professor Avrom Udovitch, and his wife, Professor Lucette Valensi, who provided links with members of the foreign faculty at Princeton University.

Writing and researching material for this book has been a rich and rewarding experience. I thank Bernard Scharfstein, President of the KTAV Publishing House and Adam Bengal, Managing Editor for bringing the project to fruition. It is my hope that others who peruse these pages will discover the joys of the ties that bind and pledge to maintain them.

Rochel U. Berman
Boca Raton, FL

Foreword

by Joy Epstein

In an increasingly global economy, individuals around the world find themselves torn between their decisions to live abroad and competing family responsibilities and cultural ties at home. Those left behind are similarly distraught that their loved ones have moved to some far corner of the world.

I am the Clinical Supervisor for the Department of Social Services for Nefesh B'Nefesh — an organization that assists Jews all over the world to fulfill their dreams of living in Israel. As someone who has also chosen to live far away from my own family, I know first hand the complexity of the decision to leave family behind, the price that people sometimes pay for making this difficult choice, and also the wonderful ways many people have discovered to help keep the ties alive. Fortunately, the options modern technology has provided enable creative connectivity no matter how far away one lives from family.

Among the recurring questions I hear in my work with immigrants are: How will I cope with the illness of a parent from afar? How will I be able to help with the care of an elderly parent? How can I show my parents that I have not abandoned them? How can I overcome the guilt I feel for not "being there" enough? Will my relationships with my siblings change? How can we continue to be a family from afar?

Most people don't think about the ramifications of distance on their family relationships when they are making the choice to move far away. Nevertheless, at some point, they will be awakened to the effect of their decision on their bonds with the entire network of family members. *Oceans Apart* comprehensively addresses both the challenges that living oceans apart pose, and the many solutions that people have found for staying connected and involved in their families' lives.

As a professional who deals with these issues continually, I responded to this book with strong feelings of identification and validation. *Oceans Apart* touches on the entire spectrum of long distance relationships that I address with the hundreds of families with whom I and my staff work on a-day-to-day basis. After reading this book, I realized this is a universal phenomenon. We hear the voices of Rajan from India, Kim from Malaysia, Rebeca from Venezuela, and so many others, each of whom had a different reason for emigrating. The experiences of such a wide array of individuals from various countries broadens our understanding of the motivations, experiences and dilemmas common to many cultures. Each of the stories shows the internal conflicts involved in the decision, and explores how each person has found solutions that work for their families.

What I loved most about the book is that Rochel Berman, herself a grandmother with children and grandchildren who live oceans apart, has supported her children's decisions and has worked at overcoming the distance. She has embraced the evolving modern technology as a means to help her to stay actively involved in her children and grandchildren's lives on a daily basis. She has also brought examples of creative ways by which people have ensured that their parents remain an important part of their own and their children's lives.

Unfortunately, some parents who were not encouraging of their children's decision to move so far away, feel rejected or abandoned. They fear that they will lose contact with their children, and will play only a peripheral role in their grandchildren's lives, if any role at all. In many cases this becomes a self-fulfilling prophecy unless the children can somehow develop new ways to maintain the relationship. I tell my clients that it is up to them to show that they want to maintain the relationship. They need to be the ones that demonstrate how it can work. Using the ever-improving telephone and internet technology to include parents and other relatives in their lives, relieves their parents of the feelings of resentment and anger that: "You have abandoned me. You have stolen my grandchildren from me."

Oceans Apart provides examples of commitment to family that was so strong that people were willing to forgo some material things and instead put away savings in order to sponsor family members on annual visits. This investment was well worth the sacrifice as it helped the entire family feel that spending time together was the highest priority.

When this happens, their relationships are maintained, and often even enhanced. I have heard many of my clients say, "We speak more frequently now about real issues than we ever did before." "We value the time we speak and we make use of it to really bring our parents into our lives and make sure they stay actively involved in our children's lives."

One of the wonderful gifts that this book offers are the "Lessons from Life" that appear at the end of every chapter. They provide suggestions and tips for making the most of relationships and for dealing with difficult situations that arise.

Creative ways to stay in touch are available via VOIP telephones, webcams and Skype. One grandmother I know sends each of her grandchildren books geared to their own comprehension level, and supplies herself with a copy of each of the books she sends. She then plans regular weekly story time with each of the children via Skype. She reports that this can be done successfully with even her youngest grandchild, who does not yet speak. With the use of a webcam, one doesn't have to wait for visits to make scrapbooks or do projects together. Even drawing together can be done through Skype.

Children in Israel involved in a genealogy project in 6th grade are required to interview grandparents about their lives, their families, and their life experiences. This is a wonderful way for grandchildren to connect with their grandparents and by using Skype it can be almost as satisfying as sitting next to each other with the tape recorder on.

Oceans Apart emphasizes the importance of visits, and why advance planning needs to be an integral part of the visit, both for the children who might come alone, and for entire families who might come together. Making plans for quality time to be spent with each individual as well as with the entire family will ensure that the bonds are strengthened and deepened through these visits. We are reminded that creating memories together doesn't have to cost a lot of money. Just spending time doing the normal everyday things together can be the most important aspect of a visit.

One area of long distance living that I am particularly familiar with here in Israel is the choice to have one spouse maintain their business/professional life in the country of origin. This phenomenon has enabled families to fulfill their dream of living in Israel without giving up on the professional and financial benefits from an established business. In this arrangement, the husband usually lives part time in Israel and commutes part time to another country. In *Oceans Apart* we meet one such couple who point out that this lifestyle only works when marriages are strong, communication skills are highly developed, and each spouse has a high level of independence.

I have worked with many of these wives and learned of the creative ways they ensure that their spouses stay involved in their lives. VOIP telephones and Skype, play an integral part in their lives. Along with keeping the couple in touch and on the same page, many long-distance fathers describe how they keep up with their children's school work using Skype and have regularly arranged study sessions to help with homework and prepare for tests.

Oceans Apart doesn't shy away from painful issues such as facing illness and death from a distance. The stories described and the various ways that people cared for and honored their parents, shared responsibilities with their siblings, gathered around the parent at the time of death, and found ways to mourn collectively as a family were particularly insightful, empathic, and touching. As we grow older and our parents age, we can all benefit from hearing other people's experiences in dealing with this difficult, but inevitable, passage.

In my own work, I have always been mindful of the fact that it is the reality of living in the 21st century that has really enabled us to remain so involved with each other, despite living tremendous distances, oceans and continents apart. I am reminded that in the "old days," leaving home often meant not seeing or hearing from the family member for years at a time, with no means of communication other than the outdated, infrequent letter or message sent with someone traveling to the home town.

The advent of interactive telecommunication and mass air travel have both enabled people to move far across the world and yet remain connected to the homes and people they have left behind. *Oceans Apart* is a wonderful and wise book that address these issues. I look forward to sharing its insights with my clients and encouraging them as well as their families to read it, as they work to maintain and strengthen their relationships with loved ones from a distance.

Joy Epstein holds an M.S.W. and has completed post-graduate training in family therapy. In 1998, she moved to Israel with her husband and four children. In 2005, she joined the staff of Nefesh B'Nefesh as the Clinical Supervisor of the Department of Social Services.